El Salvador
1979

The Civil War Escape
Memories of a Child

Claudia M. Rodriguez

Fulton Books, Inc.
Meadville, PA

Published by Fulton Books 2021

ISBN 978-1-63860-263-7 (paperback)
ISBN 978-1-63860-265-1 (digital)

Printed in the United States of America

This book is dedicated to the most supportive and role models in my life: my mother, father, sister, and brothers.

Without our Lives experiences and my recollections of growing up, this would not be possible. Your sacrifices and experiences in life have been the motivation of my professional career goals.

If you always put limits on everything you do, physical or anything else, it will spread into your work and into your life. There are no limits. There are only plateaus, and you must not stay there. YOU MUST GO BEYOND THEM.

—Bruce Lee

Contents

Part 1

The Escape

It was 1979 in Santa Ana, El Salvador, Central America, and my life was the best that I can remember. We lived in a two-story house on the outskirts of the city, and behind our house was what I called paradise. There was a mountain with lots of vivid color green trees, the jungle. I remember seeing huge big palm trees in the back near the road behind my house, which led to the mountain. During our summer days in the USA, which is winter here in El Salvador between May and October, I could hear the thunder and see the lighting from the window of my bedroom during the days and nights. I could see the giant palm trees swaying back and forth and being scared that they would fall on top of our house. I was only seven years old, and I recall my mother not being home at night most of the days because she was busy working at the restaurant she owned. So I would run to look for my father to the room next to mine in hopes that he was there. Of course, he was always there but had fallen asleep. I would try to wake him up. I would cry a lot because I was so scared of the thunder and lighting. My brothers and sister were all asleep, but I just couldn't. The thunder made the house shake and sometimes tremble that it was too scary for me to be in my room next to the window. It terrified me to see the giant palm trees swinging back and forth, and it just felt so scary.

My father would mumble finally and say to me, "Go to sleep, my daughter. It's okay. Go to sleep."

But I couldn't, and I would tell him to go with me to my room. Around 1:00 a.m. or 2:00 a.m., my mother would come home from the restaurant every night. She would find me crying and awake and comfort me and take me to bed to put me to sleep.

Every morning, our maids came to our house to take care of my siblings and me. They would get us ready to go to school and make us breakfast. Even though we were not millionaires, to us that was a good life. Being served by all these maids everywhere we went, at home, and at my mom's restaurant was nice. We also attended private school. I remem-

11

ber I never liked going to school as the teachers were nuns at the all-girl school my sister and I attended and for some reason, nuns scared me. Every day was the same routine until a bad day came. I still remember those years as the best childhood years of my life. In school, we always had some kind of event going on, and we had to perform. I used to be a ballerina, but we also had other cultural dances we had to perform. I remember parents clapping and smiling at our performances every time we had a show. It was an amazing time being a child and doing all types of performances. The nuns would also teach us how to sew at a young age to prepare us to be good housewives when we grew up.

After school, we would go to my mom's businesses, whether it was the restaurant or her retail store where she would sell different types of cosmetics, clothes, and supplies. I loved going to either one of them as I would get free toys at the retail store or free food at the restaurant. In the evenings, we would usually go to the restaurant after the retail store was closed. My mom would also pay private teachers to teach us to play instruments or to learn how to paint. I learned to play the piano at the age of five. But during the time she had the restaurant, my siblings and I would take turns playing the piano for all the customers that were there to enjoy the music while we performed. It was a very nice feeling to entertain them and to see how they enjoyed having their meals while we played.

Life was good until one day that I remember my mother telling my father that there was a problem. It was then that I started panicking. It was 1979, and a civil war had started during that year. It was getting worse. I remember my father and mother talking about the guerrillas or the FMLN group (Farabundo Martí National Liberation Front).[1] My parents would talk about it and how scared they were to get hurt during this war. At nights, I could hear bombs or gunshots far away from the house, but it was getting pretty scary. We were one of the few wealthy families in our town, and I guess the FMLN group was targeting the wealthy people in that area during that time and destroying their businesses.

---

[1] https://en.wikipedia.org/wiki/Farabundo_Mart%C3%AD_National_Liberation_Front

One day after school, I was at my mom's retail store, and I could hear gunshots and bombs getting closer to our business. I recall my mom telling her employees to close the windows and doors of the business and hide in the back. Every business in our street was closing their doors and windows. I guess the guerrillas were getting closer, bombing and destroying every single business on that block. My mother seemed very scared and worried. She turned around and told me to go to the very back of the patio and hide. I remember I went and hid behind a sink.

I would hear my mom telling her employees, "They are coming closer! We needed to take cover and hide!"

They were all praying—my mom and the employees. In my memory, I can still, until this day, hear the bombs and the gunshots and the sound of the people shouting and getting closer to the business from that day. They were throwing the bombs at the businesses, destroying them as they passed by. My mother was very scared. I guessed that could have been the end of us. If they threw a bomb to our business, we would all be dead and gone. I remember her praying with her employees that God would keep us safe from harm. Thanks to God, nothing happened to us that day.

That evening, we went home, and that night, I remember my mother talking to my father. They were always secretive about their conversations, which, in a way, was good that us, their children, never heard them argue or discuss adult issues.

The next day, I could hear them saying they were going to send one of my oldest brothers to the USA to be safe and away from the war. As the days went by, my parents kept talking that my second oldest brother was tied up in the fence at the high school he was attending. The guerrillas threatened to kill him. I heard my mom saying they tied him up against the fence and pointed the rifles to him and others and they were going to shoot them all. It was a blessing that my brother and others were not killed and escaped that threat that day.

My mother was constantly nervous and scared. During one of the nights at the restaurant, I recall my mother saying that she was threatened by the guerrillas to get killed. She told the story that the guerrillas made her and her staff get on the floor. They pointed rifles at them and said to my mother that we must escape the country or all our family members were going to get killed if we didn't leave. Everything happened so fast. The next thing I knew was that her retail business and restaurant had also been destroyed. They threw bombs at the restaurant and burned the retail store the same night that they threatened her. That all happened after she closed the restaurant and was home. We were lucky not to be there when it all happened.

In my mind, I wondered what was next and if they were going to attack her other business.

My mom took me to the site of her retail business, and there they were…all the toy soldiers I used to love to play with were all burned. All the toys against the wall of the business had been set on fire. I was so sad. I couldn't believe all this was happening to us.

Life was not the same anymore. Everyone around me seemed scared and talked a lot about the guerrillas—how they took people, adults and young children, for ransom and how they were going to business owners to ask for money or they would be dead. It was not the same anymore, and my mother, just like that, decided not to take my sister and I back to school

Every day, I would play with this little girl that lived in the mountain behind my house. She would come down and play with me. It was fun, but at the same time, I don't even recall how she came into my life. Perhaps she was a little angel sent from heaven for me to be distracted while my parents planned how to keep us safe.

I didn't see my brothers and was just wondering where they were and why they disappeared.

One day, my parents told my second oldest brother to be careful and safe. That was the day he left El Salvador to go to the United States. I didn't see him again for a few months. The situation seemed to be getting worse in our city. There were gunshots and bombs during the winter nights. It was hard to fall asleep, not knowing if we were gonna wake up alive the next day.

My nice comfortable life had ended there. What was going to happen next? Where were my brothers? Everything changed so fast in a matter of weeks, maybe not even a month. My life was shattered. I was scared. My mom, my father, and everyone were all scared. We just didn't know what the future would bring us.

Chapter 1
Antigua, Guatemala

I remember seeing my mom, sister, and me on a bus, in the middle of the night. We were going somewhere. But where was our destiny? Where was my mom taking my sister and me? Why was mom fleeing the country so fast and at night? I had no clue and just knew I was feeling scared. A few hours later, we arrived in Antigua, Guatemala. My mom's younger sister, a nun, lived there during that time. She lived in a monastery. She was so happy to see us. The nuns gave us a room and told my mom that breakfast would be ready at 7:00 a.m. They told her exactly where we should be and for us to behave at the table. We were going to be eating breakfast with other nuns and had to be very respectful to them.

The next day, we got ready early in the morning to go have breakfast with the nuns. We got to the dining area, and I noticed that all the nuns were so happy to see us. They talked to my mom and asked my sister and me if we slept good during the night and if our beds were comfortable. We told them that we actually did. Everything was fine the first night. The monastery was kind of scary though as it was an old building. I remember it being a big scary building. During the day time, they had classes for the local students. Lots of kids came to study there. They allowed my sister and me to play with them during their recess. I remember my sister telling my mother that one of the girls told her that there are ghosts in that building and nuns from the past float in the air in the hallways during the night after midnight. I was terrified of ghosts that after I heard that conversation, I was unable to sleep during the night. The days passed, and I had no clue if we were going back home soon. I thought we were just visiting for the weekend or a week. But as always, I was never told anything, probably because I was so young. I was just seven years old.

The next day, I heard my sister talking to one of the girls from the monastery. They were both thirteen years old, and their conversation seemed very interesting. I remember my sister was so curious about what the girl had told her that one night, she decided out of curiosity to get up past midnight and go walk in the hallways of the monastery. She just wanted to see if what the girl had been telling her during the day about the flying nun was true. I heard my sister leaving in the middle of the night but after like twenty minutes, came in running into the room.

I remember she told my mom, "Mom, wake up, please, please."

My mom woke up and asked her what was wrong. I overheard my sister telling her about the story of the flying nun the girl had told her two days ago during recess. She was curious to see if it was true. She went to get water to the kitchen, and on her way to the kitchen, she noticed that there was a flying nun in the hallways. She saw the nun floating in the air going toward a room in the back of the building. She told my mother that she really was floating in the air and for my mom to go see for herself.

My mom, being curious about it, also decided to go and check out the hallway. She seemed to always be into believing in ghosts and people doing witchcraft to others and even to her. My mom always told us her stories and what she believed people did to her. It was late at night, and my mom was still looking in the hallways for the flying nun my sister supposedly saw. After like fifteen minutes, she came back to the room and told my sister that everything was clear, that there was nothing out there, and that it was all her imagination.

The next day, we decided to go explore the city. Antigua is such a beautiful old town. It was once the most important seat between the Spanish colonial government between Mexico City and Lima, Peru. It is a city full of colonial ruins of churches. Many of them are old convents and monasteries but have been made safe for tourist. The monastery where we stayed with my aunt was pretty old, and that was why my sister and I were scared of staying there. We had heard before of the scary tales of the flying nuns. Other ghostly scary tales were also told to my sister about those monasteries, cathedrals, and ruins.

It was a Saturday morning, and my mom had made plans for us to go explore the city. My sister and I were excited to get out of the monastery we were staying at. The day was cool as usual. The weather in Antigua was mostly overcast. You could smell the cool air and feel the cold hit your face when you walk out of the building early in the morning. You could also smell the fresh bread from the local bakeries as you walk down the streets. Everything was closed around us, but we could see that some of the vendors were starting to set up their kiosk to sell the beautiful art they sold. Most of them were descendants of the Mayan Indians, selling their handmade bright colored textiles and pottery and more. I loved it there… I love the cute small pottery they sold. They were always my favorite. Small pots and cups, nice embroidered blouses, and cute purses—everything the indigenous people sold there was cute and perfect, which has been a collection that I keep as a memory of that city. My favorite part of the shopping was buying candy. It was so good. They sold them in the shape of the pottery and were very colorful too.

That morning after going with my mom and sister walking through the streets and looking at all the kiosks and the items they sold, my mom decided that we should go check out this old church in town because it was a ruin and she wanted to go inside and look.

I remember my mom telling my sister and me the story of the ruins and what had happened there in Antigua in the past. Approximately in 1717, people from the city believed that the earthquakes were the cause of the volcano explosions. The story goes like this: On August 27, 1717, there was an eruption of Volcán de Fuego.[2] The earthquake damaged the city considerably that everything was practically destroyed.

Central Park—*Parque Central*—is the heart of the city, with a fountain there as a popular gathering spot. To the north of the park is the Arco de Santa Catalina, one of the most unique architectural landmarks of Antigua.

---

[2] https://en.wikipedia.org/wiki/Antigua_Guatemala#17th-century_events

Antigua is noted for its very elaborate religious celebrations during Lent, leading up to Holy Week and Easter. Each Sunday during Lent, one of the local parishes sponsors a procession through the streets of Antigua extravagant with artistic carpets, predominantly made of dyed sawdust, flowers, pine needles, and even fruits and vegetables adorning the procession's paths. It is a beautiful procession to see. Kids also play with colorful eggs full of confetti. You can also hear a lot of fireworks day and night in the city for the celebration.

My mom, sister, and I finally made it to the church. It was kind of creepy. It was dark and cold inside. My sister and I were scared. As my mom was looking around the church, she kept talking to us and telling us scary stories about the place. Everything looked so old. My mom told us that underneath the church were catacombs. My sister, curious to see how we could find the entrance to the catacombs, found a metal door on the left side of the church toward the front door.

She told me, "Look, sister, here is a door to get in to the catacombs. We should try to open it."

I was scared and told her no. We might get in trouble. As she was trying to open the door, we heard some noise.

My mom, sister, and I looked at one another and asked my mom, "Did you hear that?"

My mom said yes. Then we heard a voice telling us in Spanish, "Ladies, don't touch. Don't touch anything."

We were confused and scared as we didn't know where the voice was coming from. We looked around. It was so dark, and we couldn't see. Then we heard the voice again telling us to leave it alone. This time, we heard it coming from above. We looked up, and there was a balcony. From that balcony we saw a man…however, to our surprise, it was a very short man, a midget. My mom was laughing as my sister and I were scared. It was a funny moment for my mother, but a scary one for us. We left the church, and we all started laughing. My mom said to respect the man and that it was not funny to make fun of him. The funny part to us was that we kept hearing the voice in the church but could not see him.

As we left the church, we continued walking in the beautiful streets of Antigua. I kept stopping at the kiosks to see all the cute souvenirs they sold there. I loved them, especially the ones I could eat, since I loved candy. My mom would try to buy us almost everything we touched; however, my sister, since she was a little older than me, already knew the importance of money and how hard it cost to make. So every time my mother would ask us if we wanted something, she would tell my mother no. I am the youngest of four, so my parents always spoiled me. She would buy me the candy or anything I wanted.

By the time we finished walking around the ruins and the streets of Antigua, it was time to go back to the monastery. We sort of had a curfew to go back and always had to be back for dinnertime.

We got back to the monastery and had to get ready for dinner. We prayed with the nuns to say grace before we ate. After we had dinner, my mom would stay with my aunt and the nuns to talk. We were sent to our room. I had no idea what was going on. I just knew that we had left El Salvador, our home, and everything behind (including my beloved father). The days passed, the weeks and maybe a month, before my mother told us we were moving on. We asked her where we were moving to. She would tell us the land of opportunities. We had no clue where that was.

But soon enough she told us, "We are going to the United States of America, where all our dreams can come true."

My sister and I were confused. We didn't know how far that was, but my mom knew. The nuns including my aunt had told her how we could make it to the United States. They didn't send us alone. One of my mom's cousins decided to continue the path to the United States with us. She knew Mexico City, and she was going to take us there. My mom, for a period of time, thought perhaps we should just stay to live in Mexico. After all, Mexico was very nice, and there were also opportunities there for us to go to school. But her cousin did not want that. My aunt, the nun, had told her she had to help us get all the way to the United States.

My mom was legal in the US as she had come here when she was younger. My father too. They both had green cards. My mom's cousin convinced my mom that we had to continue our travels to the United States.

Chapter 2

Mexico City

A few days later, we all said bye to the nuns including my aunt. I was sad and crying as I was scared to travel through unknown lands just us women—two women and two children (my sister and I). But the one thing we all had was faith—faith that we would make it to the United States. My brothers were already there, and so we had nothing to fear. I guess what was scary was the thought of crossing Mexico where we did not know anyone that would guide us.

We left the following morning on a bus to Mexico City. I don't remember much of the travels from Antigua to Mexico City. I must have slept most of the way. I remember we got to a hotel in this big crowed city. Lots of people and cars were everywhere. It was like the city with the most people I had ever seen. Coming from a small town, it was culture shock for me. My mom and her cousin were happy that we made it. We got to the hotel, showered, and got comfortable from the long trip on the bus from Guatemala.

That night, I remember my mom talking to her cousin. They were planning for us to go sightseeing the next day and maybe for a few days around Mexico City to the tourist attractions. The following day, we went to a very famous church in Mexico City, where the story of the Virgin of Guadalupe that appeared to a man named Juan Diego was very famous for.

The next day, a Saturday morning, we decided to walk to the church. It was not too far from the hotel we were staying at. My mom and her cousin decided to take us on a tour to the church, and as we were walking by, we could hear a narrator saying the story. It was a beautiful story that I would like to share with you.

The story is one that almost any of her followers from Mexico can narrate by heart. On December 9, 1531 (same day as my birthday), only a decade after Spanish troops had conquered the Aztec empire, a native man named Juan Diego was walking near a hill known as Tepeyac on the outskirts of Mexico City.[3] He was on his way to catechism when he heard a beautiful sound from the top of the hill. Following the sound, he came upon a vision of a beautiful woman floating in the air. She told him that she was the mother of the true God and that he should tell the bishop that she wanted a church built there in her honor. He then went to the bishop to tell him what had happened, but the bishop did not want to hear him. Juan then returned to Tepeyac, and the Virgin appeared to him again and asked him to return to the bishop. He did so, and the bishop received him the next time but still doubted him and asked him to bring a sign. Juan returned once again to Tepeyac, and the Virgin promised to send a sign the next day. Juan was not able to return that day to the bishop because his uncle fell very sick, but on December 12, Juan met the Virgin again. She reassured him and told him not to fear, describing herself as his mother, one who would care for him. She assured him that his uncle was cured and told him to go to the hilltop and gather flowers to bring to the bishop. Though it was December, he found roses and other flowers growing there, and he grabbed a bundle of them and put in his robe. Juan carried them back to the bishop. When he unfolded his robe, the image of the Virgin appeared to the bishop. When Juan returned to his uncle, he learned that the Virgin had also appeared to the uncle and called herself by the name of Guadalupe. According to the stories in Mexico City, the small church was built almost immediately and that image of Our Lady of Guadalupe was placed there. We loved listening to the tourist guy telling us the story about the Virgin of Guadalupe.

---

[3] https://www.catholicsandcultures.org/mexico-story-apparition-virgin-guadalupe

That night after our little tour in the downtown area of Mexico, my mom and her cousin were talking about the next move—if we were taking a train to the northern part of Mexico to be closer to the US border or take a bus just how we did from Guatemala City to Mexico DF. I was so young that I remember just watching TV that night with my sister as they both talked about the plan.

The next day, we walked back to the area where the church was at. I remember lots of street vendors selling all kinds of weird food that I had never seen or eaten before. They called them huaraches, sopes, and tacos. Everything smelled so good. Of course, we all had to try everything as we had never had that type of food back home. The meat was so delicious. I can still smell it until this day. That day was fun too! We were looking at all the kiosks that sold souvenirs and eating all the good tasty food everywhere we walked by in the city streets.

During the nights after exploring the city, I remember that before we went to bed, my sister and I would read some Mexican comic books. Some were not good for me because they had adult language, and my sister was not supposed to read them either. But my mom let her because they were funny. I loved to see the cartoon pictures. I remember my favorite comic books were about Archie. So every day, we would do the same thing: go to the church, pray, and then go eat and eat and eat more. My mom would buy me candies, and I enjoyed eating them. We stayed in Mexico City maybe for a week or two.

The day came that we had to continue our trip to the north to make it to the USA. I remember my mom's cousin telling her we should go to Chicago instead of California. She had a brother that lived there. My mom didn't like the cold, so she told her no and that we were going to California where we could meet my brothers. They were in California already after all. She felt that California was perfect for us as there were more Latinos living in the Los Angeles area. So their plan continued. I remember we were on a train crossing Mexico to get to the north of Mexico. I wasn't sure which city we were going to. It was just that my brother was going to pick us up when we got to the USA.

The ride on the train was not that exciting. I remember it wasn't that clean, and some of the people were rude to us, maybe because we were coming from El Salvador. We were on the train approximately one day or two. All I knew was that I couldn't wait to get to the USA and be with my brothers and also to come to this big country of opportunities that my mom kept mentioning to her cousin about.

Chapter 3

Northern Mexico

We finally made it to Mexicali City—a city in the border of Mexico and the USA. We stayed in a hotel until we waited for someone to pick us up and take us to the other side of the US! We were excited and nervous coming to such a big country—the country full of opportunities! My brother had sent someone to pick us up and take us across the border. He was working by then and could not go pick us up, so he had someone pick us up.

I remember it was nighttime, and we were getting ready to get on a van to go across the border. My sister, mom, and I were nervous as we didn't know the people picking us up. We didn't know them; my brother did. So we got on the van, maybe at 8:00 p.m. I remember the ride was like one or two hours to get food and fresh air. I remember the people stop at a viewpoint by the ocean, and I could smell the ocean breeze and see the stars in the sky. We already had crossed the border, and we had to stop to stretch. It felt so good. I was too excited. I couldn't wait to see my one brother but was told we still needed about two more hours to go before we get to our destination. That was kind of sad as I was already tired and hungry. After we stopped at the viewpoint, we were taken to a retail store. I remember it was huge, and there was everything there! I had never seen such a giant retail store in my life! This was America! Everything was here! Anything you needed and wanted could be found at this store. I was in shock. I loved it. I was sad because I knew I couldn't have everything. It cost money, and I knew my mom probably didn't have much left after all the stops and cities we had traveled through.

I remembered we walked through the store and checked out everything. I loved it! I fell in love with that store. I didn't know what it was called until months later. It was Kmart, my favorite store for many years once we got settled.

After a couple of hours of break, we had to get back in the car and go to the person's house to spend the night until my brother came to pick us up the next morning. It was going to be too late and far for him to pick us up that night as he lived far from his friend's house. So after two more hours of travel, we finally got to the person's house, and they took us to a room so that we can rest and sleep. They told us my brother will pick us up the next day. I was super excited. I was finally going to see my brother. I remember hearing my mom telling her cousin that my oldest brother had gone back home. I guess he did not like California and would rather go live with my father back home. It turned out that my father did not leave El Salvador. With the war going on, he still felt comfortable staying behind, and so my oldest brother decided he would go and stay with him too. All this I found out after my brother told my mom what had happened. But it was okay. We were still together—my second oldest brother, my mom, my sister, and me. To my mom's surprise, she found out that the daughter of one of my father's best friends was already here living with my brother and engaged to get married. It was a shock to her as she thought he was coming here to make a career and better life than the one we had at home.

My brother picked us up the next day and took us to his apartment. It was so cute where they lived but also pretty small. He told my mom that hopefully we would be getting our own apartment soon too. My mom had to look for a job so she could get the apartment. She worked very hard once she started working because she wanted us to move out from my brother's apartment. We lived with him for approximately two months. By then, my brother was married, and he decided to move out of the apartment with his new wife to another city. So my mom decided for us to stay in that apartment until she made more money to take us to a bigger home. It was a one-bedroom apartment, and she really wanted my sister and I to share a room and for her to have her own.

I was sad my brother got married and moved away from us. But I knew he was happy, and that was all that mattered. He and his new wife seemed very happy with each other. It was the nicest love story I ever heard of. I am not sure if it was because it was my brother or because they really looked so cute and happy together.

Part 2

California

Finally, it was time for my sister and me to start school here in America. We were both pretty scared as we did not speak English fluently. I was scared. Really scared. I didn't know how the kids at school were going to treat me. It was scary to go to a new school where I didn't know anyone. So here my story in America begins.

I started third grade. The name of the school was Heliotrope Avenue School in Maywood, California. I was pretty scared and very nervous to go there. I knew that it was going to be very difficult for me to make friends and communicate with them as I did not speak English. And so the first day started. And like usual, there are kids in the classroom that want to be your friend, your real friend, and there are those kids that want to make fun of you and bully you all along. In the classroom were those two types of kids.

Every morning, I would get ready to go to school. I made a few friends that lived close to the apartment, and I would walk with them to school. They were the closest friends I had while we lived there. School was hard for me to understand as I did not speak English. I can remember the teacher telling some of the kids to help me during class as they were bilingual. They had to translate for me so I can do my homework and classwork. But third grade was not bad after all. I made friends, and we got along all year long.

When I got to fourth grade, I still was having a little hard time speaking and understanding English. I can remember a few kids that used to bully me. They would make fun of me when I tried to speak the language. The teachers were Caucasians, so they did not speak Spanish, and it always made a little harder for me to understand what they were saying. But in a good way, it was good that they didn't speak Spanish because it made me communicate with them and learn the language faster. On one occasion, I remember one of the homework assignments was to get an article from the newspaper and give a brief summary about it in class the next day. I was terrified, and I remember some kids making fun of me once I got to the front of the classroom. They were making so much fun of me that it made me nervous and made me start crying. I can remember some of the kids that were my friends telling the bullying kids to shut up and to stop making fun of me, while I cried. That was an embarrassing moment, and I just didn't want to go back to school the next day. Every day, it was getting scarier for me to go to school, knowing that those kids that bullied me were going to be there once again. I did tell my mother about it, and she had to go to the school and talk to the principal so that they can put an end to the bullying.

When I was in third grade, my mom still didn't make much money, and she couldn't afford to buy me shoes. So one time that my father came to visit us from El Salvador, he cut the tip of my shoes. He said that they looked cool. I was so naive that I didn't care, and I remember going to school with the tip of my shoes cut. Now that I think about it, that was so embarrassing, but I guess I didn't care the way my father put it. I don't believe any of the kids made fun of me for that as we were all kids and were more into learning and playing during that time. To me, it is a memory that I will never forget of how poor we once were when living here in California.

From the little English I knew, I remember one day, I was sing-ing, "Row, row, row your boat gently down the stream," in class… and the teacher heard me.

She said I was very talented not just because of the way I pro-nounced English but also because I was doing very well in class. She decided I should be an honor student from that day on. So she had my mom enroll me in a special class for honor students.

My life was getting better now, and I was going to fifth grade. The challenges I went through in fourth grade were pretty rough, but I was able to survive. And even though I was still learning English and had those bullies trying to make my life miserable, I thought to myself, *I will not let them win. I will not let them make fun of me, and I will show them who I am.* From that moment on, I studied and studied very hard. Every day after school, I would go straight to our apartment and study. Homework was my first priority before going out and play with the kids from the block. I would get home maybe around 2:30 p.m. or 3:00 p.m. and, during summertime, would go out and play with the kids after 5:00 p.m. or 6:00 p.m. My sister would be in the apartment doing her homework too, while I would play outside with the kids. Every day was exciting for me after school. I really enjoyed doing my homework and playing outside. We would roller-skate, ride bikes, and play hide-and-seek. The boys loved to play hide-and-seek. I knew they liked me too. At such a young age, those boys were all into me, I guess, because I have green eyes. But I wasn't into them. I just enjoyed playing. During our summer or spring breaks, I would try to do some gardening outside the apartment. I remember, one time, I planted a potato. A few months later, there were a lot of potatoes! I was so in shock to see so many! But they were there! It was such a great feeling. I think I did that because one of my good friend's mom had like a little farm in the back of their house. They had tomato plants and other types, mostly herbs.

During the summer breaks, I would wake up late—around 9:00 a.m. or 10:00 a.m. I would watch TV in the mornings. My favorite shows were *The Love Boat*, *Gilligan's Island*, and the *Price Is Right*. By the time those shows were over, I would start cleaning the house. My sister would be in her own little world, and my mom was not home but was working. My mom wanted to make sure we had everything we needed, so she worked long hours and would come home late at night during the week. It was hard for her as she was the sole provider for us. My father stayed behind in El Salvador, and he did not help her financially. She had all the burden on her own of raising two little girls in this big country and city.

Life to me was good though. Even though we didn't have the commodities we had back home, I was happy learning English, making new friends, and living the lifestyle we had established here. One thing I do remember that was sad and brings memories is that I used to tell my sister on Saturday mornings that I wanted pancakes for breakfast. I guess we were so poor that we didn't have pancake mix; and so what my sister would do was toast bread, add butter, and put some sugar on top, and she would tell me that was my pancake for the day. I was so young that I would eat it without complaining about it. It was food, and it could have been worse if we didn't have anything to eat.

As a child coming to California from living a wealthy life was pretty hard to adapt. But my mom always told my sister and me that this was the land of opportunities and that to never give up, to strive for what we want because everything is possible here in America.

With that in mind all throughout my childhood, I decided I would strive for the best and study very hard no matter what came my way.

Fifth grade was not as hard as my fourth grade, but I still had to struggle a little bit with my English. At school, my favorite subjects were always English and math. They were the ones I scored the highest all the time. I loved doing the homework. I would never get tired. As I moved up a grade level, I was always enrolled in the honors classes. My mom was very proud of me because I was an honor student. During the fifth grade, I remember that my mom registered me to play the violin. At first, I didn't want to, but as time went by and I learned to play it, I liked it a lot. So I got into music. Learning to read the music and play the violin was so much fun. I guess I already had that in me since as a little girl back home, my mom did pay a teacher to come teach us to play the piano at home.

Chapter 1

Middle School

So I graduated from elementary school, and now I was going to sixth grade. I was so nervous but excited at the same time. I was going to meet older kids from seventh and eighth grades but also knew it would be challenging for me. It seemed not a lot of kids liked me. This was where all the bullying started getting worse for me. Some kids used to make fun of me. I guess because of the way I dressed and perhaps how I looked. I used to dress kind of weird sometimes. Well, it was the '80s look, and I tried hard to be with the fashion trend. Every day was a challenge for me. The night before school, I was looking through my closet to see what I would wear the next day to school. How should I do my hair? This was the time girls started putting on makeup. I didn't know if my mother was going to be okay with me wearing some. Just so you know, I was afraid of my mom at this age. I think most teenagers are. I never knew if she was going to be stricter with me if I asked her for permission for me to put on makeup. But one night, I decided to ask her if it was okay for me to wear some. I thought she would react mean to me, but instead, she was okay with it. However, the makeup I could wear was just lip gloss and mascara. Wow, that was nothing. But I was happy anyways. It was the age where you are just getting introduced to be a young lady. Some of the girls at school used to wear a lot. Yes, they looked like clowns to me. I always thought that being simple and plain, being yourself, shows the most beauty in you. There was no need to put too much makeup.

So from that day on, I wore light makeup and started dressing differently. I enrolled in a band in middle school. They did not have string instruments, so I had to give up playing the violin. Instead, I decided to learn to play the flute, that was a little more difficult to learn; however, I did learn to play it pretty well that the band teacher asked me to play the piccolo because I was the best flute player. At least that's what he told me.

Going to middle school in sixth grade was pretty challenging. There were girls that didn't like me and lots of boys that were after me. I think the girls didn't like me because of that. It really wasn't my fault boys liked me. I can hardly remember the exact words the kids that bullied me used to call me. I just know I used to go home and would cry in the evenings.

At this time, my sister already had a child, and she was young too. She was seventeen when she gave birth to her beautiful daughter. Seeing the life she had at a young age and being a teen mom seemed to me too challenging. I never wanted to be like her—getting pregnant young. I used to see girls in middle school that got pregnant at thirteen, fourteen, or fifteen years old. It was not good. I would tell my mom about it and let her know that I felt disgusted to see them pregnant. They were just kids like me.

My mother, during this time, had already become so independent. She had her own business where she did pretty well. She would buy me everything I wanted, take me shopping every weekend, and go eat at fancy restaurants (well, the kind she could afford) at that time! It was fun and nice, and I felt that everything was coming together just how it was back home. She always had a driver taking us everywhere. She would pay guys or ladies that knew how to drive to take us anywhere we needed to in any car that she owned. You see, my mother, besides not learning to speak English, also did not drive. She had a car accident at a young age and was terrified after that, that she decided that she would not drive.

My mom dropped out of school after fifth grade. She never liked school, and even though we came to the USA, she didn't want to learn the language either. But somehow, God took care of us. She became successful enough to support us. What I learned from her and my sister was that when I grew up, I wanted to be different than them. I didn't want to struggle. I didn't want to get pregnant as a teen.

From the kids at school that used to bully me, I was angry at them throughout middle school. But I was silent. I would never tell them anything. I would ignore them. What I learned to do best was to become a stronger person. The more they made fun of me, the stronger person I became. I wanted to grow up already! Be smarter! Succeed! Learn as much as I could and try to be my best! Everybody can do that! We don't have to let people that put us down be happy that we have failed. Instead, we need to grow and become better! Life has so much to offer that many people just don't know how to take advantage of it and enjoy it.

That's one thing I learned from my mother! Live life to the fullest while you can. Enjoy it every day! Strive for your dreams, and they will come true; and don't let anyone put you down!

Because I was an honor student at school, I was lucky enough to go to field trips they had at school. I remember that my favorite field trip was going whale watching. The teacher we had at that time was so nice, and he would explain everything in detail. It was my biology class. I loved it. I can still remember and feel the fresh breeze of the ocean until this day. It was such a fun trip with the kids from school and the teacher. Nowadays, all those extra programs or field trips seem to have been cut from the educational system. But if they haven't, I feel that every student should be able to go to field trips. It gives life a different meaning. You learn so much if you just pay attention to everything during guided tours. I suggest that any student from middle school to high school should take advantage of any field trips that might still be offered at their schools. It gives a different perspective to the meaning of life! It makes you want to strive and become someone professional when you grow up! There are so many positive outcomes that are planted in you when you go to these field trips. Most of the time, they are positive for your future career goals. Even though you are still young in middle school, it wakes up that ambition to grow older and make a change in this world. Well, at least that is how I felt about it. I am so glad that my sixth-grade teacher took us on the field trips.

I never let anything stop me from learning. Until this day, as a grown-up woman, I still love to learn. We are currently going through a pandemic in the world as you all know—COVID-19. It is a scary time for us all, but even though it's happening, I am still striving for more learning. I decided to start practicing the violin again. As a child, I did it, remember? Well now, instead of stressing, I am finding ways to put back some of that childhood talent into my life. I need to learn a Christmas song for this year. It is summer time now, so I still have time to practice.

I always feel that even if you get bullied in school, or anywhere you are having problems, you need to continue striving for better things. After all, we are all the same. We are smart. We can put as much information as we want in our brains. Computers can't be smarter than us. We can make ourselves smarter than the computers.

When I was young in my teenage years, the computer age was booming. At first, I thought I wanted to become a software developer, but it was just a bit too hard for me during that time. The coding was like a foreign language. It became too hard for me to master it. So I changed my career path in my high school year. In my senior year, I decided to take an accounting class.

Chapter 2

High School

So here we are. Finally, I was in my high school years. I was loving every day of my life. Even though I still had some bullies in my life at school, I learned to continue ignoring them. I can share with you guys though about this one incident. A guy who thought he was all tough for no reason, during physical education, started arguing with me. I can't recall what it was all about, but the one unforgettable memory I have is that at the end, he spat on my face. I didn't cry nor told any professor about the incident. But instead, I learned to ignore him. I went to the locker room and showered and changed. When it was time for us to get on the bus to head back to our high school, I just acted as if nothing had happened. Most times, ignoring is the best thing you can do when you have enemies. It hurts them more. There were also much better things to focus on during those times than dealing with ignorant kids or people that they themselves didn't know or still don't know what they want out of life. So what I did was I continued studying. I put all my efforts in studying. I studied and studied so much that the more I learned, the more I wanted to learn. I just wanted to be an adult and become someone—someone better than my mom, my sister, or people around me. I wanted to have higher education. Because of my ambition, I really focused so much with studying that I never stopped. I loved it and still continue learning all that I can until this day. To me, the books and learning were and are still my passion. I don't let anyone or anything distract me. I found out that if you focus in your dreams and you plan them ahead of time in a timeline, things will happen. All your dreams will come true! I did that in my senior year of high school. I planned my goals for ten years, and I wrote them down in a timeline. I also prayed every night, and I asked God to make them come true. My timeline was in the wall in my room next to my bed, and every night before I went to sleep, I would pray and looked at it.

I felt passion to reach my goals deep inside my heart. I really wanted to accomplish them all. I knew it was not going to be easy. I knew that because I was raised by a single mother, and I used to see her struggle to get everything she wanted for us. I always tell younger people (like you perhaps) to never give up on their dreams and strive for the best! Become better than your parents. Never forget about family but still pursue what your dreams are.

The best thing about being in high school is that you have the opportunity to learn different subjects. As you study those subjects, you can see which one is the strongest one that you like the best! Once you know which subject you like best, you can start preparing for your future. You can start researching on the field of study you would want to pursue after high school. It is awesome to learn all the subjects you learn in your younger years. Teachers, after all, are trying to prepare you for your future. I know that as kids, we don't take that seriously most of the time. We hate school. We wish we were grown-ups and worked and got paid. But the reality is that being a kid and a teenager is so much fun! All you have to do is follow your parents' advice, go to school, and learn and enjoy your vacation to the fullest! What more do kids want? I know we want to make money and buy our own things without asking our parents, but to do that, you need to get educated first. Fight all the battles that cross your path and don't ever give up! Life is too precious, and we only have one, so make the best of it.

Because I was an honor student, I was part of a group of students that went to a college during my ninth grade. I was so honored to be part of that program. It was also a great experience, and it just made me want to study harder to become someone professional after high school. Every morning, we would get on the bus in front of the high school and take a ride to the college. It was probably about a thirty-minute to one-hour ride if there was traffic. I had so much fun and enjoyed that program while it lasted. We also had the opportunity to go to USC for a week, and it was so much fun to hear the professionals speak to us on how we can have a better future if we continue our education. I kept that in my mind throughout my high school years with the hope to have a better life.

In tenth grade, I decided to enter a contest for high school students to write about a famous Cuban, José Martí. He was a famous poet, philosopher, translator, professor, and publisher, who was considered in Cuba as a hero because of his role in the liberation of his country. I won first prize from all the high schools in the state of California that wrote for the competition. However, because I was not of Cuban descent but Salvadorean, they gave me second prize. No one won first prize (well, I did). It was weird. I know my mom was so proud of me, and I was surprised that I won. I did notice back then that it felt good every time I won. So I strived for more every time.

Sometimes when we are feeling down (as kids), we are afraid to approach our parents to talk about problems we might be having at school—whether with some of your classmates or with the subjects you are studying. Our parents are here to help us and give us advice when we have issues. It's good to approach them and ask them without fear of what might be going through your life. Parents want us to succeed when we are grown-ups. They want the best for us.

As a teenager, I was afraid to tell my mother if I had problems with someone in school. I was scared of the kids that used to bully me. But I had to tell my mother so that I felt better about myself. She would listen, and she would go to the school principal and discussed the issues if they seemed to be bothering me. They would fix it, and I would be happy and be back to school with no fear. I learned from that not to be afraid to speak up. Nowadays, there are many agencies for young adults that you can call to help you with problems if you are afraid of talking to your parents. These agencies can give you positive feedback on how to resolve the problems you might have. You can get information at your schools from your counselors.

So as the year went by, during the tenth grade, I learned to drive. They used to have driving class in the high school I attended.

I remember it was pretty scary at first getting behind that wheel and seeing the students in the back seat scared. Well, we were all scared of one another every time we took turns driving but, at the same time, excited and having fun that we soon were going to drive and have a permit or license.

During all this time, my mother was working very hard. She had her business and was just too busy to spend more time with me as when I was younger. But it was okay because I was just always studying in my room at home and she was just working hard to have more money. When I finally learned to drive and got my license, my mother made me her chauffeur. By then, she used to pay me to take her to collect money from her customers. I would do that after school for a few hours during school days and during the weekend for almost all day. It was hard, and I learned from her that to have money and to buy the things you want, nothing is easy. I did that for a while. I helped my mom until I got a real job.

During that time, one of my high school friends her mom used to work in the Los Angeles garment district in one of the factories where they made clothes. She offered my friend and me to go work there on the weekends or during our summer break to show us how hard it was to make money if we didn't get a college degree. My friend and I decided to go and try it. However, to my surprise, it was hard labor! I did not see myself doing that for the rest of my life after high school! I then realized I needed to study harder, go to college, and get a real job in an office one day. But that was not going to happen any time soon. I was still too young. So I had to strategize and see what I did like and what places would hire me to work at the age of fifteen or sixteen. I tried McDonald's. It was definitely not my dream job. So I resigned after one week working there. From McDonald's, I went to work at Kmart. I liked it there, except that I had to go in at 5:00 a.m. during my summer break. I lasted working there maybe for a month. It was fun though. We got paid cash every week on Fridays. That little cash I made made me happy. I used to go shopping for school supplies or diaries to a nearby store that was called Pic N Save at that time. Nowadays, it is called Big Lots.

As time went on, I got a little older, and I wanted to earn more money. Money was like my passion. But I also knew I had to keep getting good grades so my mom and the school could let me have the opportunity to work. So I got myself a job at Domino's Pizza. I love pizza, and there, I learned so much. I liked it so much that I lasted one entire year working for them. It was a fun job. I loved taking orders over the phone and making the pizzas. The best part for me was when making the pizzas and tossing them up in the air, ensuring that when they came down, they didn't go through my hand. At the end of the night, I was also able to bring some leftover pizza home. But then, like my previous jobs, I wanted more and make more money. So a great opportunity came up. My sister was already working in an office. She was the manager there. She was like twenty-two years old at that time, and she offered me a job after school. I thought this is it! I got my dream job! I am going to work in an office. I was so excited that I couldn't wait to start working there! They used to open in the afternoons and close at nine at night. I would work a few hours after school since I was still in high school.

Life was awesome. I still was an honor student in high school, getting good grades and working practically full-time. All the kids that used to bully me where all into their girlfriends and going to concerts and school events. I loved it because finally I was left alone. I focused on myself, what I wanted, how I could reach my goals, and what I needed to do to accomplish them. I always liked to have plans of my dreams and my goals. I believe that we all should. I believe we need to write them down and, before we go to sleep at night, dream of them. I had my timeline next to my bed on the wall that was on the left side of me. Every night, I would look at it before I closed my eyes. I always prayed, and I still do! I asked God every night for my dreams to come true. But having a dream of your dreams, it's the best experience you can have. You need to picture yourself in them. See yourself on every move you make, and in the morning when you wake up, you will have a happy smile on your face too!

So it was my senior year in high school, and things were getting very exciting. All the high school events were starting, and my girlfriends and I were talking about the dresses we would wear to prom or any concerts that were happening at my high school. Twelfth grade was unforgettable.

I was having fun! Fun with girlfriends. Fun with boys. I was a big flirt! I admit it. I enjoyed the attention from the boys that were after me. I felt that there was nothing wrong with that. So even though I was focusing in finishing my senior year of high school, I still wanted to have fun with friends. In all my junior high and most of my high school years, I never ditched school. Well, I did once and went to someone's house. Kids were drinking and dancing. I thought, *This is ditching? What a waste of time. Looks too boring to me!* I guess I never liked drugs, which is a great thing. Drugs don't get us anywhere but instead get us in trouble if we do them. So instead, I told my friends we should do fun things if we ditch school.

So they asked, "Like what?"

I told them we could go to the beach or to the mountains. After all, we all knew how to drive. Most of my friends agreed with it. So on our second time ditching school, we decided to go to the beach. It was so much fun.

Ditching is not good, just so you all know. But I know that one day or another, kids miss school to go hang out with their buddies. What I am saying is, if you do escape one day, do it in a safe and clean way, no drugs or alcohol. Alcohol or any other types of drug get you in trouble in life, either when you are young or older. It is not good. We are not all perfect, and that's why I am sharing this part of my life. But it's not like I did it over and over and over again.

The third and last time we ditched school, we decided to go to the mountains to have some fun. Prom was the following weekend. We were all excited that we were graduating the following weekend. It was too fast! The four years of high school just flew by. We went to the mountain, and we were having fun. But when it was time to go home, we ran into a little problem that could have been our last time being alive! The car got out of control when we were coming down the mountain, and it was going straight down to the mountain. The car was just halfway on the border to fall down the hill. Our other friends that were in the second vehicle stopped and rescued us. We were all pale—scared that it could have been the end of our lives. The driver wanted to jump and kill himself because he couldn't believe that it could have been the end of all of us. We all supported one another. We knew that it was just an accident. We were okay, and that was all that mattered. After that incident, we all decided to never miss school the rest of the year. After all, it was almost over, and we were all going to go our separate ways. People started making their lives as young grown adults. Some went to college, some got married, and some joined the military or went to work full-time after high school.

Chapter 3

Junior College

After I graduated from high school, I was so excited! I was starting college. Going to college is so exciting. You are basically on your own. You go to class, but it's up to you if you do your homework or not. Of course, we all wanted to pass and graduate. So as young adults, we did our best to study hard and pass the classes. I was so much looking forward to finishing college. I started at California State University Long Beach. I wanted to study aeronautical engineering because my dream was to go to space. I really wanted to see the earth from above. When I went to the orientation classes and saw the hard science and math classes I had to take, it made me think if that was the career path I really wanted to take. I thought about it, and then I decided to change my major. During that time, I was dating my high school boyfriend. He wanted me to go to the community college he was attending so that we could still be closer to each other. I was so naive at that time that I listened to him. I decided to attend Cerritos Community College. It cost less money, and I could do my general classes there.

As you might recall, during my high school years, I created a timeline. I put that timeline on the wall by my bed. Everything that I had written in my timeline had started to happen by now. So now, I was in college, and I needed to think what path of education I was going to take. I had changed my major—from aeronautical engineering to becoming an accountant. So I started taking accounting classes. But at the same time, I thought, *What if I get pregnant during college? Will I still be able to attend, or should I plan a plan B in case*

I can never continue my education? Well, I always thought of having two plans in life. If one fails, maybe the second one will get you out of trouble. So I decided to get two AA degrees: one in general studies just in case in the future I decided to get my bachelor's degree and one in business administration with accounting concentration.

My first two years of college were awesome! I used to carpool with my boyfriend at that time. We always had breakfast every morning too after our first class. After my second year in college, my boyfriend had graduated and got his AA degree sooner than I did. He wanted to marry me. However, I had bigger dreams. I wanted to get my bachelor's degree. My passion was to keep going to college, graduate, and get my dream job. So I decided to break up with him.

He wanted to marry me. He wanted a family. I was not ready. But things happened when we least expected, and I got pregnant. I was twenty-one years old. I was not too happy as I wanted my dreams to come true. But even though we did what we had to do to have a family, I still continued my education. We had a big wedding. I had my son, but I never stopped going to college. Oh, and by the way, I still was working full-time. I never had an excuse not to work and go to college at the same time. Everything is possible when you plan it and you dream it.

It was a struggle. Yes, it was—being a wife, a student, an employee, and a mom. But one thing was that I never gave up. Through everything that went on in marriage, school, and work, I continued my education. I was glad I had two plans entering to college. This was the time that all was happening, but I felt sure and positive at all times that I could do it no matter what. I could reach my goals. After five years of being married and having a five-year-old son, my marriage, like most marriages nowadays, was failing. I was having problems with my husband, and it was just not looking good. We separated, and I was left alone with my son. And my mother that used to help me took care of him. She was supportive while I went to college so that I could finish my degree.

At the same time that I left my ex-husband, my father passed away. It was two stabs in the heart at the same time. I felt so depressed. I wanted to die. Even though my father was not living here in the

USA, I missed him. His loss was what made me a stronger woman. I wasn't going to give up. I wanted to graduate and be an accountant like him. The divorce wasn't going to make me stop from reaching my dreams and my goals. There was a time though at the beginning, when my father passed away, that bad thoughts went through my mind. I wanted to join the military to die faster or perhaps do drugs. At one time, I thought of committing suicide. What really stopped me from doing any of those crazy things was my son. I had gone to the army to see if I could join. My son was five years old at that time. When I came home from the army, I had a lot of brochures. I was so excited to join; however, when my son saw the brochures and asked me what they were, I explained to him. I told him that I was going to go away for a while but that I would be back. My son cried so much and told me not to go. When I heard it coming out of his mouth, it tore my heart into pieces. How could I join and leave him now? I can't do it. So after carefully thinking about it, I decided I would continue college, go to the university, and get my bachelor's degree. My father's death and my son's plea for me to stay home made me a stronger person. I can say that I was determined to continue studying. There was nothing or no one that was going to stop me from reaching my goals.

So my journey began. I worked full-time. I went to the university full-time, and I used to take care of my mom and my son financially. I would pay all the bills. It was a struggle, but I made adjustments to my life, just as how we all have to make them most of the time. We need to learn and adapt to the changes. Life is not always easy. We all go through struggles. We need to learn how to deal with them. As you might recall, I used to get bullied when I was in school. It was not fun, but I managed. Most times, we have to decide whether we ignore the problem or we try to fix it. We can try to fix it, but if it doesn't work, then you need to find other ways to solve the problem. Remember, there is always a solution to a problem. Life is as beautiful as we want to make it, but you also have to remember that our God is the one that makes everything happen when we ask from our heart. You all need to believe in him because like me, everything I have wanted in my life has come true. God knows what my heart wants, and he really has made it happen.

As I continued going to college to get my bachelor's degree, I had so many good job opportunities. The best was coming my way. My dream job! I was working at a warehouse food distributor, and I had an opportunity to work in an investment firm in Los Angeles. I was interviewed for the position and was hired the same day! The office was awesome. It was the dream job anyone wanted to have. The pay was four times of what I was making at the food warehouse. It was like God placed me there. My dream of working in a very nice building and office, surrounded by all these executive professionals. I was only twenty-six years old then. What more did I want? It was a blessing!

Working for an investment firm in Los Angeles opened my eyes for greater goals. I became more ambitious. I was still going to college, but by now, I was in the university. I was attending California State University Dominguez Hills. I would go in the evenings after work. I had graduated from Cerritos Community College with my two AA degrees and successfully transferred. Life was getting good. I loved my job and my life by then. While working for the company, I was tasked to travel to the corporate office in Chicago. Sometimes, we would go to the New York office. I remember though my first trip was to Washington, DC. This was one of my dreams—working in the corporate world. It was amazing and wonderful—by far, the best experience in my life. My bosses and my coworkers were all supportive and great people. I learned so much from them. But my boss was the best. He taught me how to enjoy life to the fullest. He would always mentor me and take me out to eat in nice fancy restaurants. He would tell me how much I should spend when eating in fancy restaurants. He trained me to find the best deals so I could, one day, travel the world. He showed me how I could enjoy life to the fullest without a man in my life. He was awesome.

I believe that when you surround yourself with professionals growing up, it motivates you to become more successful in your career goals. It also depends on the passion you feel as a person to make your dreams come true. Four years had passed working at the firm. My sister was living in San Bernardino at that time, with her two young children. My mom and my son lived with me, and we used to visit my sister almost every weekend. And I remember she told me, one time, why don't I move to San Bernardino so I can buy a house closer to her? I was making good money at that time and also paying too much rent in Los Angeles area. So I decided to move to San Bernardino with my sister until I found a house. At the same time, I was going through a divorce. My life was so complicated like many adults during these times, but it was harder with divorce and also going to classes at night after work. I had to transfer to California State University, San Bernardino, to continue my career path since I was moving there and was not giving up my studies. I had to get my degree and complete it, and there was no one nor anything that was going to stop me from completing it. I was only like two years away from graduating, and I had to finish no matter what. I was finally divorced, and I felt that I wanted more. I wanted my dream car—a Mercedes—but then I thought a house is a better investment. So I started searching for a house. It was so exciting that I was actually buying my own house.

So I searched and searched to buy my home. Coming from a third-world country and knowing how expensive it is to live here in the United States, I made a plan. Now this plan was to buy a house that I could afford the payments and still be able to save money at the same time. I always think of the future, and as a math major, I learned to always ask myself two questions: *Is it a need or a want, and can you live with it and adapt to it with or without it?*

I think you should always ask yourselves those questions. It helps build and work with our current situation and also helps us develop a plan for our dreams to come true.

I graduated from the university finally! And life was great! I had bought my house. I had my dream car, and my son was already ten years old. And we both had survived with my mother after my divorce. I still used to commute to Los Angeles to my job. I had to do it. It was important for me to keep my job as it was my only income to support my mom, my son, and myself. Life is not easy, as I mentioned a few times. As kids, we sometimes take things for granted or don't even make an effort to better ourselves. We need to listen to our parents because they know that life is not easy when we become adults.

I believe that if you have any problems as a young adult at school, with friends or even your own parents, you can always find solutions to those problems. That is one thing I have learned in life from my experiences. My sister actually was and still is one of my motivators to never be afraid to move on, to ask for what you think is fair in life, and to not be afraid to ask your parents or your bosses in the future for something that is beneficial to you and perhaps the company you will work for. All they can tell you is a yes or a no. The best thing about it is that whatever response you receive, it's either for your benefit or to learn a better way to approach your solution to any problem you might have. Most of the times, we win, so you should never be afraid of asking your parents to talk about a problem that is bothering you or never be afraid to ask your boss for something that might be beneficial for both of you. Always think positive. Always believe in your dreams because there is a Greater Being out there, the Creator of everything, that always hears us and knows what is in our hearts. If you believe in him, everything and anything is possible. I have experienced that myself for many, many times during my young adult life growing up. Miracles do happen. But they start with you and what you believe to be true.

So let's continue with my story. I bought my house. I had my car, and life was so good to me. At the firm I used to work in Los Angeles, my bosses there were very good to me. They saw how smart I was, and they pushed me to continue my studies until I graduated. Remember I was going through a divorce, and the times were really tough for me. But being surrounded by professionals made it easier for me to focus in my education and be able to finish the degree.

I was commuting from San Bernardino to Los Angeles to work back then. It was, at first, a one-hour commute, either by train or driving. For the first three years that I lived in San Bernardino, the commute did not bother me. I made a lot of friends in the train, and it was really fun, especially because the majority were professional employees like me. Everyone wore suits to work and carried their laptops in the train. When I was going to the university and working in Los Angeles, I started taking my laptop in the train too, and I would do my homework in the morning and afternoon commutes. I would also study for my exams if I had any.

I loved my train time, and until this day, I still miss it. I loved being surrounded by professional people that used to give me positive advice about life and how I could make it better. I learned from them and my bosses to travel and not be afraid to go eat to a fancy restaurant.

That was the best part of growing up after high school and college. You work with professionals, and they teach you on how to enjoy life. I am not rich, and I never was, but because of the right guidance, I learned to make the best of life as long as I have a job.

You must learn to choose wisely your friends. I was bullied as a kid, remember? But I never let that stop me from reaching my dreams. I am picky and always was picky when choosing my friends. I didn't have many, and I still don't have many friends. But I do have a few that I selected that are really close to me. Those are the friends that I treasure and will treasure forever. It's okay not to have too many friends. Sometimes when you are alone, you have more time to plan for more goals in your life. It gives you time to think of what it is that you want to pursue next. You can also study more and concentrate better when doing so.

During my teen and twenties, I always traveled a lot. I would save money and go visit relatives in Canada. From work, I would go to Chicago or New York. I went to Miami, Detroit, Seattle, Portland, and Texas, just to name a few. But my ultimate goal was that one day, when my son turned eighteen and I was going to turn forty, I wanted to travel overseas somewhere. I planned that for many years and couldn't wait for the day to come.

I hope that my story has motivated you in some way and that you find the courage to talk to your parents when you need any type of advice or are having a problem, not to be afraid to confront people that bully you throughout your path in life, and to strive for your dreams through good and bad times no matter how bad it looks. Just remember that no matter what you are going through, there are many agencies that you can seek help and advice from. Talk to your counselors at school. They will guide you to the right agency if you ever need advice.

Best of luck with your career choices and always strive for the BEST that is in YOU!

Acknowledgments

I would like to thank my loving mother, Elba Rodriguez, for her unconditional love, encouragement, and contribution to my book. Thank you to my family for the joy they all bring to me daily.

I would also like to thank the following people: Nana Danquah, for mentoring me and pushing me to never give up. Laronte Groom, for encouraging me to never stop writing.

Bibliography

1. https://en.wikipedia.org/wiki/Antigua_Guatemala#17th-century_events
2. https://en.wikipedia.org/wiki/Farabundo_Mart%C3%AD_National_Liberation_Front
3. https://www.catholicsandcultures.org/mexico-story-apparition-virgin-guadalup

About the Author

Claudia M. Rodriguez was born in Santa Ana, El Salvador, Central America. She has a bachelor's degree in business administration with accounting concentration from California State University of San Bernardino. She is interested in becoming a politician and has served as a city commissioner for the city of San Bernardino and a member of other governing agencies in the city and nearby cities. She loves to travel internationally. Going to different countries and learning about their languages and cultures motivates her to continue her learning. She is passionate about the writing and speaking of the many languages. Being a mentor to younger adults and seeing them succeed makes her life fuller of life as she was once mentored and has successfully accomplished everything she wanted to as a child by being surrounded by professionals.

Claudia enjoys living her life to the fullest along with her son, daughter-in-law, and siblings. She still resides in beautiful Southern California in the Inland Empire area.

Unfortunately, Claudia's mom passed away on December 2020 because of COVID-19.

CPSIA information can be obtained
at www.ICGtesting.com
Printed in the USA
BVHW030827091021
618601BV00007B/110

9 781638 602637